Ain't These Sorrows Sweet
poems
by Lauren Scharhag

ROADSIDE PRESS

Ain't These Sorrows Sweet

Cover Art: Beth Barnett
Editor: Michele McDannold

Roadside Press
Colchester, Illinois

In loving memory of

Robert Anthony Boleware
and
Isabel Marie Martinez

Contents

Sweetness

Sorrows

Things My Uncles Made in Prison

Two out of three sons spent most of their lives in prison.
Both former altar boys, they were more devout
when they were inside; they talked to their mother more,
making collect calls, and quoting scripture in their letters,
which she kept in a drawer along with a green plastic rosary,
yet another carceral memento, and Polaroid portraits of them
in their prison blues, taken by inmate photographers.
I think of their hands, holding the pen, fingering the beads,
growing old before their time, fashioning objects
that they intended to set loose, like doves at a funeral.
The gifts arrived, packed carefully in newspaper and cardboard,
metal folk art made with old horseshoes, bolts, and washers;
drawings of Christ, ballpoint on yellow wide-rule;
wooden picture frames carved with hearts;
pendants on leather cords; a lighter case because
she still smoked Kools; and a music box shaped like a piano,
its interior lined in mauve velvet. She kept the latter
on top of her dresser. Its steel and brass movement
played a tune I can't remember.

Sorting the Beans

When I was a little girl,
Bisabuela would have me sort the beans,
a good task for small fingers,
sifting through seed bodies,
smooth and speckled as songbird eggs,
picking out pebbles, picking out shriveled or broken bits,
while she chopped onions and prepared the masa.
It seemed the TV was usually off while we worked,
which meant it must have been during the lag
between *The Price is Right* and afternoon talk shows.
She would tell me how her family in Texas had been so poor,
they hadn't even beans to eat.
They'd had nopales, the occasional armadillo.
A younger brother was lost to smallpox.
These were her earliest memories, dim and fragmented.

I've tried to look up the history of her hometown
but the articles don't say much before the 1880s,
when the railroad came. To hear them tell it,
there was nothing before then,
just vague references to hunter-gatherer tribes,
any one of which could have been ours.
Bisabuela was only three when her family came north.
Her father died on the way. So for her, too,
there was nothing before America.
This is the way of diaspora: Get assimilated or get discarded.

We'd soak the beans overnight in the old enamel pot,
also speckled. The next day, we'd have frijoles and tortillas,
pork chops if we could afford them.
I tasted time in each umami bite. I tasted 15,000 years.
The same salt and protein and fiber
that nourished all those generations, that multiplied their cells,
also nourished and multiplied mine.
My bones and teeth and tissues are beans and corn.
I can still feel the slide of sun-warmed legumes in my fingertips,
taste cactus crunch, the red pork flavor of Hoover hogs.
I taste golden petals, and though I am not full-blooded,
I am full.

Faded Ink

My uncles all had prison tattoos: crosses, praying hands,
sacred heart Jesus, la Virgen de Guadalupe,
la Anima Sola. I wonder if they used ballpoint pens,
melted Styrofoam, soot mixed with shampoo,
or something even more crude, just asking for infection,
hepatitis, HIV. One of those uncles has died. He'd been
the last to relinquish his criminal ways, had spent
the better part of four decades behind bars, but in this,
he was foremost among his brothers, in this, the last
was indeed the first. I'll admit, it was his face I often pictured
whenever, in religious instruction, the nuns referred
to the unnamed thieves. In the casket, he wears a suit.
His grandchildren lean over the sides and poke at him,
fascinated by his new hollowness, while I wonder what his ink
must look like now, how the iconography must have faded
beneath his wool and linen sleeves, how they constituted
his last earthly garments just as much as double-breasted
pinstripes; how the children were right, that we were viewing
an empty vessel, a gourd lacquered in cellblock blue,
and what awaits it all, what comes of all stories writ in skin.

Sweat

My grandparents
did not believe in air conditioning. They had
a window unit, but they never turned it on.
My grandmother would be at the stove all day,
melting manteca, toasting chiles, hot tortillas
at every meal, huevos rancheros, papas y chorizo,
beans and rice, fideo, enchiladas, gas burners
always on high, the whole house fragrant
and scorching. She kept the front and back door
open to allow a cross-breeze, a cool cloth
around her neck, and that was enough. Grandpa
was the same, puttering around in his shed,
in the garden, working on his Caddy, brim
of his hat pulled down low over his eyes, happy
as a pair of mythical fire creatures
in their element, raised in the shadow
of volcanoes and the breath of deserts, weaned
on habaneros. They didn't even wear shorts,
while we sat outside on the porch swing, in
cut-offs and tank tops, and sweated, waiting
for Lacho from the next block to come
with a wrench to open the fire hydrant, waiting
for the ice cream man's sweet mercy,
and perhaps this is why Grandpa died
in summer, he wanted to be buried
under the sun, and Grandma died
in winter, but wanted to be burned.

Maundy Days

My great-grandfather, eighty-four,
with scleroderma and dementia,
would sit still and obedient as a child

while my mother trimmed his nails,
his eyebrows, even his nose hairs.
She'd genuflect to do his toenails.

He spent his days confused and suspicious,
but he was always happy to see her.
He always called me by her name

when I was there to babysit him,
allowing my great-grandmother
some time out of the house.

I like to think that maybe, between the two of us,
mother and spectral daughter,
we added some comfort to his end,

down to 90 pounds and only able to wear sweats
because they were easier to put on over his feeding tube.
Later, when it was his wife's turn,

she stood naked at the kitchen sink, not shy
since we're all women here, more lucid
than he'd been, even if she'd lost most of her English,

still watching *The Price Is Right* on the old 20-inch.
My mother would bathe her with a washcloth,
the bar of Dial soap in its usual place,

a swan-shaped soap dish,
which sits now in my mother's bathroom.
I remember the brown body,

heavy and shapeless with age,
crooked hands gripping the counter for balance.
Afterwards, there was lotion, Suave,

a kind they don't make anymore.
I used it myself then, because I liked how it smelled,
lanolin, I think, and Vitamin E,

and how she sighed with relief, at being clean,
at being moisturized, at being cared for.
Again, my mother on her knees

with the nail clippers, not holy herself,
as none of us are, but performing a holy act,
the TV behind her on mute,

but we all knew what Bob Barker was saying,
extolling the chosen with the fervor
of a televangelist to *Come on down,*

and we, though many, are one body,
spouse and spouse, parent and child,
living and dead, host and contestant.

Tangled

My grandfather died in August. The only black
article of clothing I had was a wool turtleneck,
which my mother insisted I wear. We fought about it,
because it was going to be 98 and humid.
She said respect was more important than comfort.
I was at the hospital when he died. I had never seen
anyone die before, and when I realized he'd stopped moving,
a terrible sound exploded from my throat, half-sob,
half-cry, all primal. I couldn't stop thinking about
that violent and visceral response. Sitting on my
bedroom floor, in my teenage white cotton underthings,
hair wet from the shower, trying to untangle
the rat's nest of chains from my jewelry box,
trying to extricate the gold St. Christopher's medal
he'd given me, hands and wrists a blue tangle of veins,
rivers and tributaries my soul to traverse, trying
not to think of lowering his remains into the tangle
of worms and roots and darkness. *Dear St. Christopher,*
protect me today in all my travels. At the graveside,
sweating and swaying beneath the summer sun,
the priest delivering the rite of committal, VA volunteers,
ceremonial rifles on shoulders. When the 21-gun salute
shattered the afternoon, I fainted. *St. Christopher,*
carry me safely to my destined place, as you have now
carried him to that farther shore. I sip its cool darkness.
Amen.

Starlight

1989 cities, Tiananmen and Berlin,
and my own humble metropolis,
before people knew the necessity
of green space, the moon was as close
to nature as we were likely to get.
Evenings on the patio beneath the orange glare
of sodium arcs, days of concrete and exhaust.
I used to get excited when I saw an apple
in the grocery store, with a leaf still on the stem,
curled and brown as old parchment.
A teacher scolded me for handling
the class hermit crabs too much.
I was fascinated by such life.
Our parks were just squares of grass,
baseball diamonds, maybe an oak.
Squirrels chittered and titmice chirped
from the powerlines. Strays prowled
the alleyways. In vacant lots,
copperheads lurked in the overgrowth,
and sharp and rusty things,
and the invasive wild morning glories
that overtook the chain link fence,
common knotweed choking the yard,
and dandelions, and gravel. An open
fire hydrant was our river, the public pool
a chlorinated sea, and the starlight
reflected off the water in the glass
that I drank.

Profesora

She was from a small
Missouri town. Learned Spanish
at junior college. Moved to a city.
Taught indifferent high schoolers
who mocked her behind her back
for her orthopedic shoes, thick-soled,
white when they were new,
but always dusty, well-worn
from summer excursions
to Madrid or Oaxaca or San Juan.
In the Plaza Mayor,
a pickpocket tried to steal
from a student and she
beat him off with her purse.
She wore straw hats over
her curly hair. She ran
the Spanish club, selling churros
at lunchtime to raise money
for war orphans in Guatemala.
She brought us homemade paella.
I imagine her now, retired,
taking senior salsa classes,
ordering her baila shoes a size up
to conceal the orthotics,
and weeping
over children in cages.

Two Inches

My mother went to the doctor.
He told her she's lost 2 inches off her height.
She's always been a petite lady, and nearing 70 now.
2 inches doesn't seem so very much against the span of years.
2 inches seems immense against the span of years.
Yes, it's a large paperclip, a sewing needle, a golf tee.
Yes, it's the diameter of a billiard ball.

But her high heels used to be higher than 2 inches.
I remember the many pairs: versatile black pumps,
knee-high leather boots, bright red stilettos,
the clear Lucite open-toes we called her Cinderella slippers,
the strappy silver pair I borrowed for prom.
Now she wears flats.

Her hair used to be teased higher than 2 inches,
so many afternoons spent in beauty parlors
with a magazine and a pink helmet of perm rods,
so many mornings in front of the bathroom mirror
with a set of hot rollers, a hair pick, curling irons,
and cans of Aqua Net.
Now she has the obligatory older women's haircut:
short, sensible.

The dangly earrings that swept her shoulders,
longer than 2 inches.
The cigarettes she still smokes, 4 inches.

She was 26 when she had me.
I am already so much older than she was when she had me.
We pass through the days like a funnel, not realizing
how it gets smaller and smaller towards the end.
The average vagina is 3-7 inches deep.
It stretches to accommodate a baby.
Women gain anywhere from 10 to 40 pounds during pregnancy.
Breasts rise and flatten like topographic events.
We are small and large at the same time.
We ping-pong back and forth like Alice
at an All You Can Eat Me buffet.
She put me on my first diet when I was 8,
and now, she wonders why I hate this body so much,
how hard I work to lose 2 inches off my waistline.
When they teach us we should always make ourselves smaller,
this is not what they meant.
We know that's not what they meant.

But notches on a ruler, notches on a belt.
It all starts to look the same.
When we die, they say we lose 21 grams,
an even tinier unit of measurement.
What is 2 inches of soul?
What is the infinite?
The years whittling us down
until 2 inches is a crack you can fall through,
until 2 inches is an abyss
we're gaping at each other across.

Emotional Labor

The first time I heard someone say the phrase,
I thought of placenta. I thought of a woman
sweating and cursing in the stirrups, preparing
to deliver—what? Because I mean, yes,
labor is always emotional, isn't it? They say
natural childbirth results in a faster recovery time.
They say. I'm not sure it's worth the tradeoff.
The epidurals don't knock you out, the twilight sleep
is an artifact of our grandmothers' time, and there's
still the afterbirth to contend with, and choosing a name,
and formula or breast, and tubes tied or untied, back
on the pill or IUD or
or
or

But that's not what they meant.

They meant carrying something else entirely,
a burden that doesn't end after nine months,
an umbilicus that no scissors can cut, a perpetual
toil and aftermath that began even when we were
practically in the womb ourselves, taught that it's
our job to be selfless and nurturing and thoughtful
and accommodating, to see to everyone's needs
but our own, baking birthday cakes and wrapping
presents (and, of course, we did the shopping, even
if the card says *Love, Mommy and Daddy*), plan the party,
clean and decorate the house, knowing that we'll be

the ones to take it all down again, knowing that we'll be
the ones picking up torn streamers and discarded cups,
knowing that we'll be the ones doing the dishes, knowing
that we will bear the brunt of diapers and walking the dog
and we will have to figure out the bedtime schedule and
research preschools and then get them there on time and
make the playdates and enroll them in soccer and buy them
cleats and remind our husbands that their mother's birthday
is coming up next week and there's no thanks, of course,
it's just what's expected of us and if I told you all of it
I could fill volumes with the schedules and calendars and
menu plans and shopping lists and to-do lists that are constantly
running in my head because these aren't just my things, you see,
they're yours and the kids' and my parents' and your parents' and
coworkers' and that's to say nothing of the workplace dynamics
and oh God, is this depression postpartum, or am I just
fucking exhausted, even as we ask you again if you've assembled
the crib yet, then asking you why we even have to ask.

And you ask why I'm upset.

Is

for I.M.

I know we were never close,
and yet,
I knew you
when you truly were
that twinkle
in your mother's eye.
When she and I used to
play dolls together,
I caught a glimpse
of how she would one day
cradle you,
nurture you,
cherish you.
I knew you
when you were still
blooming inside her,
a clenched bud,
like the hibiscus that grew
in the yard
of our great-grandfather,
(your great-great-grandfather).
All we girls could be
those blossoms,
skirts of lavender
and a sunny,
bloody center,
occupying the same branch.

I saw her fight
a custody battle for you
across years and a thousand miles.
I watched her take a second job
to pay the lawyer,
waiting tables in a seedy strip joint
45 minutes out of the way,
so tired she was afraid
she'd fall asleep at the wheel
on her way back to you.
Then I got to watch you grow up,
sporadically,
a toddler here,
in pigtails and pink dresses,
a tween there,
worrying over boys and acne,
a teen,
getting your driver's license.
I couldn't believe it
when she told me
that it was your turn
to be a mother,
much less that you'd gone.
How will we ever
become accustomed
to this past tense?
How will we bear
your mother's eyes—
the spark that's left them,
but never her heart.

(Or ours.)

We hold your child now,
a tiny fire
that we will tend,
and warm ourselves by.

Mother's Day

Not a day in mid-May, but late August.
Not a day of tea rooms and flowers
but of body scans and pat-downs,
she comes,
all the way from Houston,
almost ten hours,
she comes,
eighty-three years old,
her walker granted dispensation
to pass through those hollow metal doors
into the visiting room,
where they will be given an hour.
She manages the trip
every few months;
he's been here twelve years.
Eight more to go.
He's seen so many men
come in and go out;
some who've kept in touch
take his mother to lunch
whenever she's in town.
They take her shopping,
show her the sights.
What bonds of brotherhood
these brothers in bonds
come to know.
In the morning, they will
take Mother to breakfast,

check her oil and her tires,
and see her off.

She and the son of her womb
both wonder
if she will still be here
when eight years is up.

Sisters in Mo(u)rning

I look forward to
riding the bus
in the morning
black woman driver
mostly black women
passengers.
I'm a big believer
in black girl magic
trailing the scent
of cocoa butter
down the aisle
their warm greetings
their camaraderie
exchanging dishes
both empty and full
admiring each other's outfits.
I know I am the outsider
and I envy this
instant sorority they have
wherever they go.
One morning,
I hear the driver talking
matter-of-factly
about a family picnic
and her nephew's funeral
both being held Saturday.
"They killed him," she says.
The passenger nods

says that she, too,
lost a nephew
this past week
that she too
has a funeral Saturday.
Then they go on
talking about
recipes
and hats.

The Clock-Drawing Test

Aunt Joan
can't draw
a clock face
anymore.
When presented
with a circle,
her numbers sit
in a slag heap
along the bottom,
the way time
must feel to her.

When she gets dressed
in the morning, she puts on
two or three shirts,
shorts over pants,
or else, comes down to breakfast
in her Ethel Merman swimsuit.

Sometimes, Aunt Joan
remembers.
The other day, she remembered
that all her siblings are dead
and cried the whole night through,
having lost them all over again.

Aunt Joan's clocks
leave no room for hands,
no way to note the hours.

The doctor says,
*Kids these days don't know
how to tell time
by a regular clock anymore.
In 40, 50 years' time,
they will have to come up
with a new test.*

I say, *Maybe by then,
they will have cured
this disease,
and there will be
no more need
for blank circles.*

El Chingue y Chingue

On the boulevard, I wrap myself
in the colors of the picado flags
against a winter sky,
the scents of the taqueria
bringing me home,
the faded Virgin of Guadalupe mural
in the alley, the blue wall where
San Martin Caballero rides with the angels,
the house where my grandparents
lived as newlyweds.
An abuela holds forth
on the nature of el chingue y chingue,
brandishing her cane for emphasis
as her grandson runs around the tables.
Finally, when the barbacoa is eaten,
and all that is left are
a few stray leaves of cilantro,
discarded shards of onion,
there is nothing to say but
Bye, Abuela.
Bye, mijito. Hasta mañana.

Christmas Fudge

She rises even earlier
on Christmas Day
to begin preparing:
farm table laden with ham,
scalloped potatoes, hot rolls,
pies, fudge;
small gifts neatly wrapped.
Then she waits
beside the fire,
watching the road.
Outside, snow falls
on the vanishing prairie.

Flores

When Abuela used to tell me about Mexico, she would
always talk about the flowers. On Avenida Tulum, I am
just another tourist browsing the fruit stands and strip malls,
but with every blossom I see, I hear her voice: dahlias
and passion flowers, birds of paradise, pineapple sage,
laelia orchids, frangipani, beds of agave, even the clusters
of seagrape on the shore whisper, *Remember me.*

When I return to tallgrass prairie and feed corn, when
the August sun has scorched the land to straw and dust,
I do not forget, even as I struggle to reconcile that to this,
her humble garden of tomato plants, the chain link fence
sagging beneath the weight of purple trumpet vines and morning glories,
the ragged robin roses swallowing the porch. Not even a lawn,
but a tangle of ground ivy, foxtail, and dandelions. How she
regretted having the old elm tree cut down, robbing the yard
of shade. The alley cats she used to feed sunning themselves
on the patio. Descendants of those cats roam here still, rolling
in the same river loam where we scattered her ashes.

When the monarch butterflies drift through our bluffs and
bottomlands on their way down to Michoacán, their wings
the color of marigolds, the flowers of the dead, surely they
carry some of this with them, binding place to place, flood plain
to flood plain. They carry her with them. She has become
a part of this land, this place of sunflowers and butterfly
milkweed and white hawthorn blossoms, and they carry her,
on flame-colored wings, home to Zamora.

First Blood, Last Blood

I was more upset
by a particularly violent
expulsion of a baby tooth
when I was 9.
It was one of the last to come out,
so it wasn't the novelty
that I found so shocking,
but the quantity of blood,
and I was a latchkey kid,
alone in the house.
So I pressed a cool, damp cloth
to the fresh vacancy in my mouth,
and watched *Tiny Toons*
until my shoulders stopped shaking.

The next year, during a tornado warning,
my class took shelter
in the girls' bathroom,
and we were embarrassed by the way
the boys stared, with frank curiosity,
at the tampon dispenser on the wall.
We'd never seen anybody use it,
but word had it that Amanda Harper
had been sent home from school one time
because she'd bled through the seat
of her Jordaches, and everybody knew
that Tamika Williams started way back
in third grade, swear to God.

The year after that, mine started.
It was a snow day in January,
which was lucky. On any other day,
I would have been sitting in social studies.
But I didn't think about that at the time.
I didn't think about
the snow white/blood red connection.
I wasn't even sure what I was looking at:
a little rust-colored stain on my underwear
that hardly looked like blood.
I spotted the rest of the day,
and was relieved when it stopped.
I did not have my period again
until late that spring,
and I bled and bled and bled,
for three weeks. I had to sit on towels.
I had to get a doctor's note to be excused
from swimming in gym class, and then,
I was the girl always getting sent home.

I was sixteen when Pearl, Mississippi happened.
There was talk of not letting us carry
our backpacks to class anymore.
I told the principal flat-out,
I have a heavy flow, sir.
If I can't carry a backpack,
I will walk around these halls
with a pack of Kotex.

It took 14 years for doctors
to figure out or even believe
there was something wrong with me.
They just didn't understand
how something so small
could affect so much.
For God's sake, honey,
it's just your period, one told me
after ruling out a miscarriage.
It can't be that bad.

It took another year for them
to come to terms with the idea
that some towels
must be thrown in,
that not every vase holds a flower,
that, unlike baby teeth,
there's nothing to fill this gap.

But I don't sit on towels anymore.

Here Be Dragons

Here is the block where
I was first catcalled
by an adult man.
I was 11.
Here is the city pool
where an older boy
chased me into
the ladies' locker room
where I hid until
my mother came
to pick me up.
I didn't go back
that summer.
Here is the vending machine alcove
where a group of boys
cornered me during
a forensics tournament
when I went to get
a cup of coffee.
So many locations
and tableaus,
so many scenes of
so many crimes,
so many sites
of trauma.
These are the places we carry,
the cartography of our lives,
a terrain of wounds.

Memory charts no course
through rough seas, and these
are the spatial relations
we dare to traverse.

A Seat at the Table

Men sit in the other room.
I am not a part of this conversation.
They talk about drinking and sports.
They talk about hunting.
They talk about war.
I am left out of this conversation.
They talk about cars.
They talk about the time they got drunk
and crashed a car
or crashed a war.
I am stood up for this conversation.
They talk about politics in a way that no one else does.
They talk about guns. They talk about justice.
They are the heroes of every story.
They expect everyone to be in the know, even though
I am bye Felicia'ed when it comes to these topics.
They talk about fathers, the wholeness of better men,
the bygone eras.
They talk about women, but only piecemeal.
What women have done to them.
What women do for them.
What women ought to do for them.
What women ought to do.
They talk about the hot, unattainable girls,
the crazy girls, the babymamas.
They talk about the strip joints and the red lights,
where they've been both patrons and bouncers.
They're shocked—*shocked*—that

the eighteen-year-old exotic dancer
is only interested in them for the tips.
Mostly, they talk about what women look like,
mounted on canvas or pedestals or on screens,
smiling or cooking or just jogging by.
All of these activities are obviously for them.
Finally, I barge into that room and I speak.
I say, *this is what a woman's life is.*
I say, *these are her experiences.*
I say, *these are her thoughts.*
I do not raise my voice.
I make no demands.
Still, they look at me blankly.
One of them offers to buy me a beer.

Virtual Cloister

It's not even the dick pics that get me.
They're in the same category as old-timey flashers
prowling public spaces in trench coats,
no doubt enjoying the breeze against their balls,
dry-humping at shadows.
Dick-pic senders seem to expect nothing.
It's all one-sided, a solipsistic affair.

Nor is it the ones who invite me to sext.
At least they're up-front about it. Mostly.
They might lead off with something like,
You have a nice smile,
(My pictures are almost invariably from the neck up
to discourage more explicit compliments)
then quickly segue to the request
for tedious, sticky fumblings
and they're not even as charming
as Hannibal Lecter innuendos.

No, it's the ones who slip into my inbox
by striking up conversation.
Young men rush to impress me with their vast knowledge.
(They never ask if I'm already acquainted with the subject.
In fact, they ask me nothing about myself.)
If we were talking together in person, I guess,
they'd preen and flex their muscles,
like birds of paradise showing off their dance moves.
Older men love to reminisce about their travels,

their wars. They tell me about their dogs.
They pat me on the head (virtually)
and dispense advice like, *Appreciate the moment.*
Before you know it, it's gone.
and *You ought to wear your hair up.*
And I wonder how old they think I am,
or why they think they're qualified
to tell me I "ought to" anything.
Then come the implied sighs,
the, *Oh, how I wish I had someone.*
It would be so nice to come home
to a good woman.
I love a good massage—both getting them and giving them.
I don't know if they're drunk or if, somehow,
they've never heard the sound
of their own voices.

And then, there's the lone woman who says
she'll show me her tits if I show her mine.
I think about it. Tat for tat.

Then I add to my profile, *No DMs, please.*

Estate Sale

The drawer I opened last,
with your costume jewelry
and your compacts,
that Coty Airspun powder you'd
been buying since the 60s,
your cigarette case and hairspray,
your keychain,
your loose buttons and shoelaces;
the pieces of you
that no one ever takes.

Eyebrows

My grandmother lost her eyebrows
circa 1977. Her eyelashes, too.
She tried to light a cigarette
off a gas stove burner and *whoosh*.
By the time I came around,
she liked to joke that she'd adopted
the Whoopi Goldberg look.

Now, my mother is going the same route,
but she didn't burn hers off.
She plucks them, very thin and uneven,
giving her a perpetually surprised expression,
like she's been shooting Botox.
I didn't say anything because
I didn't want to hurt her feelings,
but she's asked me if I know anything
about eyebrow tinting. I, who have never
been into cosmetics, am exactly
the wrong person to ask.
"My eyebrows are going white," she said.
"That's why I started plucking them."

She and my grandmother both
started to go gray young,
started dyeing their hair young.
They always liked their makeup
and haircare products anyway,
so it was a matter of pride for them

to take up the gauntlet early.

As gray hairs start to sprout from my own scalp
and I slide into my mom jeans,
I wonder what my struggle will look like,
what casualties will arise,
what things people won't point out,
hoping to spare me.

High School Reunion

At my twenty-year,
I look at people
I don't know anymore
(not that I ever did)
and think of how,
in the hothouse of childhood,
they had all seemed
so much larger than life.
Our parents and teachers, too.
I wonder if I ever
looked that way
to any of them,
and I think of how time
cuts us all
down to size.

The Skinner Box

The experiment involved
some pigeons, some seed,
and a box. Pigeon pecked
a lever on the box,
the box dispensed a seed.
But if the box gave
the bird a seed every time,
the bird would grow satisfied,
lazy, pecking only
when it pleased them.
If the box gave them a seed
randomly, then the birds
were far more diligent,
hoping that this time
this time, a reward
would be forthcoming,
and the act of pecking
becomes prostration,
their faith granted
the occasional boon of
two or three seeds in a row.
But if they gave the bird a seed
only a few times and then
never again, the bird might
peck itself to death
chasing a dream of satiety.
Granted, pigeons are not
the smartest of birds.

I see you, standing there,
with your pocketsful of seeds.
I will not stoop. I will not
bloody my beak, hoping
for what you might bestow.

The Sound Barrier

Thirty years in broadcasting with a specialty in sound editing, he used to complain about the poor audio quality of movies and TV. A life-long tinker and putterer, people would bring him electronics to repair, his basement shop littered with wires and old cathode-ray tubes and ham radio guts. He restored an antique wind-up phonograph he inherited from his grandmother, polishing the oak cabinet, replacing the mesh. He plays for us the shellac records, ragtime and Bessie Smith and "Old Man River," the music still clear as center orchestra seating. I'm not sure if he was ever interested in the music itself or just the quality of sound. We always had top-of-the-line stereo systems, but I never knew him to attend a concert where he wasn't wiring up the mics. He never turned the radio on in the car or had an extensive CD collection, (Glenn Miller, movie scores, Engelbert Humperdinck, Nat King Cole Christmas. That was pretty much it.) Though I do remember hearing him sing in the shower once, James Brown.

Now, I watch his face at the dinner table, contorted in frustration, unable to keep up with our conversations, not wanting to keep asking us to repeat ourselves. I have never asked him what his favorite sounds are, if he misses bells or crickets or the rain pattering softly on the roof. I know he remembers the night of the shelling in Da Nang, his father's 21-gun salute, his son's first sax solo, yelling at me to turn down the noise that 16-year-old me called music. My voice was one of the first things to go, the higher pitches flitting from his audial grasp like frantic doves. I try to convince him to text me, but he's too old-fashioned for such things. For a while, he just kept cranking the TV up louder and louder, until it was giving Mom banging headaches and she insisted that he stop. He doesn't read fast enough for close captioning, so he bought a pair of wireless headphones, blasting the sound directly into his already-shriveling eardrums.

I remember his mother's same descent into silence, or what I assume is silence, like the stillness of snowy winter nights, sitting off to the side at family gatherings, hands folded, resigned to just watching. Stress and isolation become panic attacks and he won't start a journal or do yoga or meditate or any of the things that they advise you to do to relax. Men raised on World War II stories and *Gunsmoke* and stiff upper lips have very particular ideas about what constitutes sissy behavior.

At a catfish joint, he orders a shrimp basket. The server asks, *Fried?* He says, *Yes, I'd like fries please.* And she says, *No, it comes with hush puppies. Do you want FRIED shrimp?* and he says, *Yes, fries and hush puppies.* And from there, it devolves into a version of "Who's on First?" but with cornmeal batter, and I laugh loudly and inappropriately, a laugh he cannot hear. He always said that I sound just like my mom, and if he's lost my voice, he's lost his wife's too, and I think about how he used to keep a bottle of her hand lotion in his desk drawer to sniff when she wasn't around. I wonder what he does to remind himself of the fading notes, what keepsakes he has squirreled away in shoeboxes and workshop organizer drawers, next to the broken-down amplifiers and subwoofers he's determined to revive.

Tomcat

Once, our house got robbed.
When the thieves were done raiding our electronics,
my jewelry box, even the pantry,
they did not bother to close the door behind them,
so my housecat got out.
I like to imagine he had a wonderful,
wild night in the woods behind our house,
drinking the night dew,
cavorting with the fleet-footed creatures,
maybe even a romantic interlude or two.
I didn't have to wonder long.
He came home the next day with ear mites,
the kitty equivalent of crabs.

Lucy's Last Days

Renal failure, the vet said.
A condition we knew too well—
that you knew too well.
You don't really get something like that
unless you've gone through it,
and I'd only gone through it second-hand.
You knew what it felt like to live at the mercy
of tubes and needles.
When you got your transplant,
we thought we were done—or at least,
granted a respite of many, many years.
But now, it's dialysis all over again,
the feline equivalent:
subcutaneous fluids for hydration
and to flush waste products from her blood.
The vet tech shows us how,
but we just don't have the heart to do it,
to grab the scruff of her neck and jab the needle in.
So we tried taking her to the vet every day,
45 minutes both ways,
and she already hated car rides.
The treatments were supposed to make her feel better,
but they never seemed to.
She continued to barf and pee everywhere,
especially in our bed,
at least twice while we were in it,
necessitating 2 a.m. sheet changes.
Our bed had always been her favorite place.

It got to the point where we got an old blanket
to use as a protective cover,
just as we once bought only cheap comforters
that could be thrown in the wash
from where you vomited or dribbled dialysate.
I kept asking, *Don't you think it's time?*
And you kept saying, *I can't. I just can't yet.*
I guess letting her go
felt like some kind of defeat to you;
where you didn't give in before
to the thing that could have killed you,
now you find you have to give up
a little piece of yourself after all,
that we are left once again
with unused needles and bags of fluid,
along with an empty cat tree.

Jack & Lucy

I keep feeling soft thumps
on the edge of the bed at night.
Startled from sleep,
I raise my head and look
but you are not there.

I am still picking your fur
from the fibers of my clothes.
The towels in the laundry basket
retain the indent of your form.
Some of my books were mauled by you
in kittenhood, covers still dotted
with little tooth and claw marks,
a sort of feline Braille.

I touch them and recall
you pushing your head
into my palm.

Our time has made me--

I am loveless and adored.
I am empty and full.
I am lonely and never lonely.
I am joyless and overjoyed.

The Urn
for Lucy

Originally, I had planned to scatter your ashes.
I thought I'd take you back to the neighborhood
where your mother must have roamed.
I thought, after so many years a housecat,
you might like to be free.
On a selfish note, I was also thinking how
in fifty years or so, my poor relatives will have to come
clean out my house when I am dead, only to find
my many jars of former cats.
"Poor, crazy auntie," they'll say.
"What will we do with all these cat ashes?"
But now, I find I don't want to let you go after all.
So I am choosing an urn for you.
I realized home is where you'd want to be,
high up on the mantel, where you would
most definitely be dozing
if you were still here,
in the flesh
and fur.

Valentine

Today, I ate the last
of the Valentine's chocolates
you gave me.
The sweetness is fleeting
and February is
so very long.

motley

we saw him at a comedy club
he'd starred in a film that was popular
when we were kids
and while his set was about other stuff
he still humored us and did the funny voice
said the line
if he had any other good jokes I couldn't tell you
I only remember the line
because like everyone else in the audience
that's really what I'd come to hear
and when he was wrapping up
he mentioned he was also a visual artist
and after the applause died down
he went offstage and sat at a table
beside the paintings he'd brought to sell
his expression demeanor everything different
a whole other person
not the 80s one-hit wonder
nor the working comedian in a frayed sports coat
nor even an actor
but the real him
a galaxy of abstract colors
and I was one of maybe three people
who stopped to look mostly to be polite
I remember one piece a black and white checkerboard pattern
strewn with spheres that might have been marbles
or might have been planets
and I thought again of 1988 and how this man

was a time traveler
because I swear I had a Trapper Keeper
with that same design
and I understand how the audience
wants to keep you in one lane
and all you want to do is become a pinball
unstuck from the continuum
pinging between actor comedian artist
all none you
and no doubt a multitude of selves no ticket will ever
buy us admission to

Plastic Flamingos

After the divorce, my father strewed the front lawn
with plastic pink flamingos. I'm sure he was
a John Waters fan. I'm sure he did it because he knew
how my mother would hate it: metal spikes ruining
the turf, gaudy ornaments overshadowing her white spirea,
her purple verbena, the mulberry tree. I remember
the shock of my first weekend visit, at finding this house
was no longer my house, this room no longer my room,
bare but for the old twin bed, and dents in the carpet
where my dresser and play table once stood. (Of course,
all my stuff was at the new apartment, including my new bed,
but still, I expected everything to be as it was.) Soon,
my swing set would be removed from the backyard,
the pergola my parents had built together taken down,
the clematis unwound from its cedar beams. When
our old dog ran away, neither of my parents bothered
to retrieve him from the pound. My father tried getting a cat,
but it, too, ran away. Everything disassembled, everything
emptied for the house to sell, until there was nothing left
but spirea in need of pruning, a sidewalk splotched purple
from mulberry-eating birds, and a lawn pocked with holes
where the polymer flock briefly perched, before they, too,
were banished in the name of curb appeal.

Anisomelia

i.

We were nine, and it was
the age of MASH and paper fortune tellers.
Choose a color. Choose a number.
Close your eyes. I will draw a spiral
until you say stop.

We unpopular girls sat together
in the lunchroom,
huddled like birds
on an electrical wire,
all part of the same dispirited flock,
playing our pencil-and-paper games.
Being seen together was
slightly less embarrassing
than sitting alone.

We put a ring on a piece of string,
or better yet, a strand of hair,
and recited the alphabet as it spun.
The letter it landed on would be
your future husband's initial.
We wished upon lost eyelashes,
consulted Magic 8 Balls,
chanted *Down in the valley*
while we jumped rope.
At recess, we kept close

to the school building.
We didn't want to risk
being noticed.

But even as we tried to fade
into the bricks
all we thought about
was escaping
this present.

ii.

She came mid-year,
the girl with one leg
shorter than the other,
weak and withered as an old twig.
Her clothes were hand-me-downs.
She wore those metal aviator glasses,
too large for her face and already out of style.
(I wonder if those were hand-me-downs too.)
Now I wonder if her family was poor
because they were spending money
on expensive orthotics, or possibly saving
for a life-altering surgery.

I can still see her,
walking to the bus stop,
dragging that cudgel of a shoe.
If she was out sick from class,
she'd ask me for the homework.

She knew I wouldn't be cruel to her,
(which doesn't make me kind).

She couldn't jump rope with us.
She was excused from running in gym class.
She never wanted to play MASH.

The world had already taught her
the distance between what is desired
and what is.

iii.

When I pass the old playground
I still wonder whatever happened to her.
I wonder if her short leg
ever caught up with the other,
and I think, if it didn't,
what pain she must live with,
the tilted pelvis, the perpetual limp.

But if it did, I think about
her dancing.
I think of her finally
turning eyes towards tomorrow,
drawing spirals on a piece of paper,
using shoelaces from an old shoe
to spin futures for herself.

Mansion. Dream job. Soul mate.
It is decidedly so.

Water Street

It's midnight and the snow has started
on Water Street and we are sixteen and
curfew has come and gone and our faces
are freezing but we don't want to go
home yet. We walk, hands crammed in
our coat pockets, through the last dying
scents of the late-night coffee shop,
day-old biscotti and the smoking patio
where hipsters suck cloves and cheap cigars
like depressed writers on the ends of shotguns
and tailpipes. We walk through the bar
parking lot, classic rock jukebox thuds
the night like a heartbeat, like my heartbeat,
all youth and small-town longing. One last
Christmas tree on the curb, brown needles
and tinsel, the fading smell of pine resolutions
buried under the bad habits we have only
just begun to cultivate.

Monarch Funeral

When we were kids,
my little brother would bring
ants and spiders inside
and call them his pets. He cried
when Mom stepped on them or
sprayed them with Raid.
When we found a dead Monarch butterfly
in the garden, we had a funeral for it.
We said the Lord's prayer,
laid wild violets on the tiny grave.
Now, I see him care for his children,
how tenderly he holds them,
leads them to the park.
He plants a garden.
He has plans to build a chicken coop.
I wouldn't be surprised if he had
a bird feeder or two.
He wants to share with his family
the beauty and fragility
of winged creatures.

Home for Christmas

After the first frost, all the shelters
brace themselves. Volunteers start
planning warming stations in gymnasiums
and church basements. They're stacking in
donated gloves and socks, space heaters and
Sterno cans. They set signs out on sidewalks,
warning of the deadly cold. Good Samaritans
leave blankets on park benches, put boxes of
coats out on doorsteps. On Facebook groups,
people check up on their houseless friends.
I think of the year my father lived out of his car.
It was in San Luis Obispo, which boasts 315 days
of sunshine a year, and how we would go
for months without hearing from him. Now,
would he reverse his flight, running inland
from fire and ash? In my neighborhood, people
break the locks of our apartment buildings and
hunker down in the basements, among
the storage units and industrial hot water heaters.
Outside, the snow begins to fall, season of the refugee,
of Black Friday sales and Advent. No stranger bedfellows,
Salvation Army bell ringers in front of stores where
management has posted No Loitering signs in the
parking lot. On the speakers, Charles Brown is singing
the holiday blues. Burned out encampments in
railroad yards give no scent of myrrh, and despite
all our efforts, come morning, there will be blue
angels under bridges and in the alleyways,
and we will say, they've been called home.

Prayer for the Excommunicated

somewhere outside Osceola
prairie lightning coronas grain silos
quicksilver violet
air so humid raindrops
vaporize as soon as they touch
febrile ground igniting
silt and cornrow
shaggy hillocks of buffalo
stand as one with big bluestem
diners selling bison burgers
by the quarter pound
livestock trucks thundering past
flash of horn
tails dangling listless out the slats
the damp give of fields beneath hooves
a distant memory
rising moon a blood stain
fading as it climbs to rust
to burnished copper
we count wayside shrines
with white crosses and plastic flowers
the excommunicated gathering
in the false light of all-night
gas stations where we purchase
lottery ticket devotionals and partake
of roller grill hot dogs and machine
dispensed coffee like every day is
the last supper and where every

bathroom mirror reveals a ghost
looking back.

Theoxenia
a cadralor

1. Mammogram
There is a locker room where I get undressed, leave my clothes
folded and hung in a steel box. Don the pink gown. My breast flat-
tened
between two plastic plates, fileted and butterflied, served up on a bed
of radiation.
I await judgment.

2. Cowbirds
Pastures on either side of the highway throng with yellow-legged
cattle egrets.
In medians, they trail mowers, catching grasshoppers churned up by
the blades.
Perched on the backs of bulls, picking ticks off hides. Sated, pure
white bodies
unfold themselves skyward, to return to the wetlands.

3. Fukushima
Alarmed by reports of mutated daisies,
you bring me a bottle of iodine tablets to protect
the delicate twin lobes of my thyroid. You ignore
the aspartame-laced drinks I consume, the Red Dye 40 snacks.

4. Hospitality
Our apartment on Cathedral Square was an island adrift on a sea of
indigence.
They'd break into the lobby to have a place to sleep out of the cold.

We'd leave packages of food on the low wall flanking the tow zone,
like an offering. You never know what form the divine takes.

5. Henderson Beach
I leave the water and peel off my suit to find kelp and sargassum
garlanding my skin, green and brown cursive
marking me with the language of the deep.
These legs, like everything else, are temporary.

The Pottery Shard Graveyard

Behind the art school there is a
pottery shard graveyard
where students consign unsuccessful ceramics
pieces that broke in the kiln or sad first attempts
or would-be masterpieces someone carelessly dropped
there's even a sign commemorating the spot
accumulation of untold semesters and community courses
fragments of vases that will never know flowers
cups that will never know lips
and bowls that will never hold soup or pinecones or seashells
or some of those mass manufactured decorative ball things
even figurative pieces that will never grace someone's mantle
a heap of jagged edges like
the shattered dreams of artists made tangible
some are even still mostly intact
such patterns such glazes
a testament of hands
I wonder if someone comes periodically
to cart all this off to the city dump
it can take pottery up to a million years to biodegrade
our imperfections outliving us by a geological age
I want to gather up the pieces dust them off
and turn them into something
I don't know what just something
I want to whisper to this broken bouquet
it's all right, darlings, I wasn't good enough either.

Vacillant

This is my heart
on a string,
the yeah, no,
I mean, no, yeah.
Mind on a string,
back-forth, up-down,
pink-gray yo-yo
of desire and mood,
but the body—
the body swings
only one way,
forward-forward.
A bird breaking itself
against glass,
forever-forever,
but for you, my lips
incapable of no-no,
only heaving myself
at what is solid,
praying that
these wings
are enough.

Contradiction

I sharp-dull. I upward fall.
I crash-land. I unman.
I freezer burn. I indifferent yearn.
I hurry-plod. I even-odds.
I visible dark and
bull's eye best
when I miss the mark.
I soft beat. I forever fleet.
Ain't my dirty neat?
Ain't these sorrows sweet?

Sweetness

Homemade Wine

I never tasted my grandfather's wine.
I just remember his postage stamp of a yard,
not an inch wasted with a vegetable patch,
an herb bed, a tool shed. I'm sure he would've
kept chickens if he could, but they weren't
legal in the city limits in those days. Still,
he raised enough to keep the window
ledges lined with ripening tomatoes
all summer long, arbol peppers drying
in bunches by the stove, the yerba buena
that he never bothered to steep but plucked
fresh, stuck in his jaw like a plug of tobacco,
and chewed. He spat green. The grapevine
a lush cloak over the back fence, shielding
the property from the trash-strewn alleyway,
dusty red bunches we were not allowed to eat,
reserved for vinifying. Inevitably, Catawbas
swelled and dropped, wrinkled, split, for bees
to light on. It's possible that his mother started
the tradition. They arrived in the States just in time
for Prohibition. What was there to do
but brew her own beer, set up a still—
why not make wine? I could only too easily
imagine him tending the same vine
for forty-five years, coming to know each
coil and stem the way he knew
the neighborhood. I remember the buckets
and straining cloths, his stained-red hands,

glass gallon jugs crowding the store room,
corked and left to ferment, an inch of
sugar and yeast at the bottom. By the time
they were ready, the porch swing had been
put away, the vines withered, the garden dead.
But the chilies were hung, the jalapeños
jarred. We'd entered the time of poinsettias
and Three Kings bread. I was too young
to partake, but the sharp scent of it
reminded me of mass. My aunt would come
and they'd sample it together, clinking glasses.
I imagine it must have tasted like summer.
They'd agree, it was sweet.

Home

a cadralor

1. Abuela's House

Beside the old rotary phone, the Aztec warrior, in heavy Talavera ceramics,
keeps his perpetual vigil over the body of his beloved princess,
their bridal chamber a tomb. Home is where the heart is, even after
it's stopped beating. A Sacred Heart Jesus tapestry dominates the bedroom.
In the kitchen, a gimme calendar from the panaderia is tacked
over the washing machine, day-old conchas in wax paper, a lingering scent
of onion. Tortilla dough kneaded and ready to roll out for tonight's dinner
rests in a steel bowl. Bottles of aspirin and blood pressure medication
in a row on the windowsill, along with the last of the season's tomatoes.
If our family had a sacred heart, this house would be it.

2. The Butterfly Festival

Swallowtail caterpillars, black and red, nestle in our palms. Chrysalis boxes filled
with pupae in various stages of emergence, leafy greens and golds and browns
spun from the silk of their own bodies, walls of shed skin, site of transubstantia-
tion,
the changing of the whole substance, liquefying to become. Platters of fruit entice,
winged feasters pulsate gently in puddles of juice. We eat homemade ice cream
from a vendor stand. They're here every year, as dependable as the saffron-winged
monarchs' migration. It's always strawberry for you and toffee for me. We lick
the drippings from our wrists. In the outdoor enclosure, a blue morpho lands
on the brim of your hat. I wonder what it's like to live on sweetness and air,
to have every branch and sprig a suitable bed for spinning dreams.

3.   Please Be Sure to Visit Our Website

My abuela's neighbor, Jose, does odd jobs for her. In the evenings, she cooks him
dinner.
They eat and watch TV together. At the end of *Sabado Gigante*, the announcer
exhorts viewers to visit their website. Abuela turns to Jose and asks, "¿Que es 'dot
com'?"
"Es por la computadora," he replies. She nods as if she understands, this woman
with an eighth-grade education, born before television. As far as I know, she never
touched
a mouse or a keyboard. The homiest of homebodies, she couldn't bear to be away
from her kitchen and her cats and her garden for more than a few hours. The
internet,
like biochemistry or literary analysis or Nicomachean ethics, is a foreign country to
her,
one she has no desire to visit. We scattered her ashes in the back yard. On my
computadora,
I write poems about her, and will continue do so until I am ashes to be scattered.

4.   Thank You, St. Jude

When my brother was six, he was hospitalized with a high fever.
Abuela pinned saint medals to his pillowcase.
When he got better, she took out an ad in the classifieds:
Thank you, St. Jude, for your intercession.
When Abuelo died, the prayer cards at his funeral did not invoke St. Jude,
but Christ and the 23rd Psalm. I carried that card in my wallet for years,
reassured by the idea that there will come a time
when we have no need for intercessors,

when being desperate and directionless ceases to matter.
En la casa del Señor, habitaré para siempre.

5. Flood Myths

For the first time in my life, I'd moved away from the river. So, naturally,
that's when the flood came, the deluge overwhelming our sump pumps, all the
things we lost
in soggy heaps out on the curb. We'd known this house was a fixer-upper,
but no amount of paint and wiring can resurrect some domiciles. Home isn't a
place
but a concept, an elusive state, like enlightenment or salvation. Creation began
with a flood,
its waters to devastate but also to cleanse, both hell and high water,
endlessly consuming and resuming, as the caterpillar digests itself in its chrysalis
to emerge on sodden wings. I'll never stop seeking this nowhere place, part
dream,
part memory, all Zhuangzian dilemma. There, we will talk of alphas and omegas,
plant zinnias and milkweed, and become ghosts simply because there's nowhere
else we'd rather be.

Dusk

When the lilacs end,
fireflies constellate
in the dying fragrance,
lighting the white viburnum.
On the patio,
my mother drinks
sticky-sweet wine.
Black gnats, undaunted
by cigarette smoke,
circle the rim.

The Chainsaw

When I was a little girl,
my grandmother had the old slippery elm
cut down in her back yard
so a new fence could be put in.
I sat out on the stoop to watch the men work.
A bit of metal flew from the chainsaw's edge
and landed on my sock.
I picked it off, not knowing it would be hot.
I ran inside and ran water over the burns
on my thumb and forefinger,
amazed at the pain of something so small.

Now, when I think of poetry, I think
it should be like that:
hot, gleaming steel.

All the West Side Girls Love Lou Diamond Phillips

Summer of '88 and *La Bamba*
was released on VHS.
Us West Side kids
had found our idol.

Before that, we got excited
whenever Speedy Gonzalez
appeared on our TV screens.
There was an old Chevy Chase
film my mother loved mostly
for the sassy Mexican cook
with whom she shared a name,
Aurora, and we loved anything
with Cheech Marin. If there were
other bits of Mexico in pop culture
at the time, I'm hard-pressed
to think of them. (Desi Arnez
was Cuban. Also: black-and-white.
No, thank you.) But we held them
to our hearts like talismans.

Mexicans were still exotic back then
in the way that Italians were exotic
in 1905. My friends didn't know
what a tamal was. When they came
to dinner, they tried to eat it
husk and all. The only Mexican restaurants
in town served tacos in store-bought shells,

and everything came with a side
of refried bean puree, smothered
in white cheese that was like a mockery
of queso fresco. But suddenly,
everyone knew the song, "La Bamba."
They played it everywhere,
at the supermarket, at school dances,
and even the white girls agreed,
Lou Diamond Phillips was so cute.

He wasn't even Latino,
but we loved him anyway.

My tío made bootleg copies
for everyone and we watched it
over and over. We knew
all the songs, every dance move.
We re-enacted them on the front porch,
using a broom as a guitar, a hairbrush
as a microphone. We were amazed
that someone could sing in Spanish
and sound cool, none of the warbling ballads
or cheesy corridos heavy on the accordion
that we knew from our abuela's records.

We girls started wearing our hair
in high, 1950s ponytails, tied with big bows.
Our Catholic school saddle oxfords
were suddenly stylish. The boys either
combed their hair into pompadours

or wanted black leather jackets
like Bob. Now, thirty years later,
my cousin still thinks he's Esai Morales,
roaring around on his motorcycle,
and I can't hear "Sleep Walk"
without getting choked up.

Stand and Deliver came out
that same year, but a math teacher
isn't nearly as sexy, and we had to wait
ten years for *Selena*, for Jennifer Lopez
to come with her nalgas and spangled bras.
(Also not an actual Mexican,
but we'll take what we can get.)

Oxtail Soup

In a little Tex-Mex dive
outside Houston,
the server brings me
oxtail soup
braised with beef tendon,
corn and chilies,
tortillas,
each bite taking me
back in time
through Cordoba and its
bloody bull rings,
through Moors and mosques,
all the way to Rome,
where the poorest and roughest
dined on tripe and tail.
So many miles,
so many lifetimes
I hold in my mouth,
feel glide through
the blood-brain barrier,
washed down
with Tecate.

The Ice Cream Churn

You associate your grandfather
with the wooden churn
the way you associate him
with books and overalls
and a drill-sergeant temper,
flash of cane, rattan rapping
its tattoo on your skull if you didn't
change the channel fast enough
to spare his eyes the offending
colored person on-screen. Slave-owning
a poison in the blood that four generations
still hasn't washed out. Meandering
north and west, but circling back
to visit his father's mammy
in the hills of Old Dominion.
The way his pockets rattled with change
from working laundromats.
He introduced you to
Old Mother West Wind,
and in the summers, he made
ice cream in the shade
of the back porch and let you
pour in the rock salt. Surely
your grandmother must have
scalded the can and the dasher,
surely it was her bottle of vanilla,
but he mixed the milk and sugar,
layered in the ice, turned the crank

until his arm met resistance.
He wiped away salt water
beading the top. He lifted out
the metal quart and served it.
Plain, of course.

Comfort Food

Stage 3

Manageable for a time, they say, with diet and medication.
First, they take away salt. Avoid pre-packaged anything.
Labels can be deceiving, so double- and triple-check.
Even low-sodium is too much sodium.
We are still so bewildered by the diagnosis,
we barely stop to think about how strange it is,
that such an essential thing could spell harm for you.

Then, they take away potassium, and there goes
the salt substitute. We say goodbye to corn, tomatoes,
cucumbers, broccoli, leafy greens, mushrooms,
bananas, oranges, chocolate, so many things.
We soak potatoes for at least an hour.
There are lots of tomatillos, which we learn
are not in the nightshade family, and therefore safe,
lots of pesto and salsa verde, lots of
popcorn balls and Rice Krispies Treats.
Marshmallows are the only sweet you can have.
(It will be many years before we can stand them again.)

For the first time, you crack a cookbook.
On good days, you start experimenting.

Then comes the steroid-induced diabetes,
the Cushing's Syndrome, your head so enlarged,
you frighten your nephews when they come to visit.

You can no longer manage the stairs.
Your body hair falls out. You shake.
Even your feet swell so you can only wear slippers.
At Christmas dinner, you sit at the table with us,
but do not eat. You aren't really here.

Stage 4

If you ever hit Stage 4,
it must've only been a pitstop,
a border-crossing into some
unimaginable territory
where the rest of us can't follow.

Stage 5

End stage.
Months pass in a blur
of hospital beds and transfusions,
needles and tubes, and pills upon pills.
The weight melts off as the nausea overtakes you.
Now, facing the long haul of the transplant list,
we have time to consider these essentials.
Nothing could have prepared me for the horror
of watching someone who is unable to eat.
I research all the tips for cancer patients:
setting the table with flowers and linens,
cooking your favorite foods, popsicles, drugs.
You were a vegetarian in the time before, and now,
they expect you to take at least nine ounces

of animal protein a day. So I buy shakes.
We make big batches of egg salad.
(A trick bulimics know:
if it's going to come back up anyway,
best stick to soft things.)
On the rare occasion that you have a craving,
I run out and get it for you.
If you eat half, I consider it a victory.
Marijuana is still illegal, but someone
brings us a joint. At last, you eat.
I don't care about the law.
You eat.

Transplant

With your new abundance
of time, you watch cooking videos.
You start with bread.
Before I know it, you
are turning out beautiful loaves.
In three years, we find
there's nothing you can't do, no dish
you can't master: baguettes,
pillowy croissants, arepas,
chocolate babka, Three Kings bread,
homemade pizzas and pasta, sushi,
dumplings, and biscuits the way
your grandma made them,
roasted pork belly and braised short ribs.
For Valentine's Day, you surprise me

with a filet and lobster tail.
For every holiday, we happily gift you
kitchen gadgets, welcoming you back
to a world of appetite. Every artist knows
that sometimes, you have to die
in order to create, and you have died
several times over. But now, my love,
you live, and not just on bread alone.

You live.

Confection

Summer, and almost two seasons
into the pandemic. Like many,
I'm spending a lot of time
in the kitchen. At the moment,
there's vanilla ice cream in the freezer,
peach cobbler in the oven,
my house scented with cinnamon
and sweet fruit and buttery streusel,
and I realize I must not take
my sense of smell for granted.

I knew a guy once that had a very
poor sense of smell. I don't know
if he was born that way or if it
was something that happened to him
gradually. You'd think it would
hinder his enjoyment of food,
but on the contrary, he could
eat anything. Taste is rooted in smell.
Since he couldn't really taste it,
flavor simply wasn't important to him.
He'd learned to appreciate texture.
He could throw any combination
of vegetables and condiments
into a bowl, nuke it, and call it good.
Sometimes, I envy this total lack
of particularness, but he would not
be able to smell this cobbler baking,

and I, having lived sweetness
in full, both the bitter and the pure,
would not give it up, as I would not
give up coarse ocean salt crusting my bread
or peppers that sting the tongue like nettles,
portobella umami and tart lime.
The guy I knew also had
a terrible memory, and memory, too,
is linked to the senses.

I want my nose. I want my tastebuds.
I want my lungs. I want dessert.
I want yesterday. And tomorrow.
I eat the cobbler, already dreaming
of future confections.
I am careful not to burn my mouth.

Watermelon

like the summer days themselves
we chomp its pink sweetness

down to thin rinds /
short pale nights

doused with salt to draw out
a bit more juice

half-believing wives' tales
about seeds implanting themselves in our bellies

making of our spines and throats a stake
hairy leaves unfurl on tongues

unquenched, we reach
for the next green orb

split us open. it's taken root
in my duodenum

darkness calling to darkness
unable to distinguish

my depths
from the earth's.

Skinny Dipping

the first time i went skinny dipping
i was alone at the pool it was close
to midnight and unable to resist the lure
of topaz water shimmering against
summer darkness i shimmied out of my
suit for just a few minutes because I
wanted to know what it felt like to let
the night caress all of me then I put
the suit back on went inside and
washed the chlorine from my hair.

Forever Home

As we stand still, it's only natural
to want to make our homes feel larger.
The local news tells us the shelter
is empty. We adopt two from a rescuer,
their tiny bodies barely taking up any room
at all in the single pet carrier. Suddenly,
the house is messy with catnip mice
and balls with bells inside that go ringing
up and down the hall day and night,
scratch posts that fail to entice them
away from the sofa, and a long, hide-and-seek
tunnel made of cloth and hoops. There are
strings to dangle and breakables we endeavor
to protect. They go running to the door when
the FedEx driver knocks, and I must keep them
from darting out into the steel-and-concrete
unknown. They leap at moths fluttering at windows
and stalk bugs that get in through the chimney.
They find the smallest specks of I-don't-know-
what in corners and under furniture,
and bat them across my previously clean
floors. They follow the path of the sunbeam
from window ledge to carpet, to bed, like a
holy processional, chase points of light that wink
from my phone screen. All is new. All is wonder,
their little faces unadulterated with it, mealtime
and playtime equal sources of boundless joy.
They loll and stretch and offer up their bellies

for scratching, purring their feline hosannas. Amber
and emerald eyes slow blink. By night, they sleep
curled against us, perched on the curve of a hip
or nestled into the small of a back, leaving
no question as to what makes this place home
for them. Nor do we question what makes it ours.

Destin

White sand, black bikini,
stretchmarks shimmer
across her lower back
as she bends, lifts the baby
onto her hip,
and strolls out into the surf.

Women Alone

After the divorce, we moved to an apartment
on the other side of town. I loved our new home.
Even at five, I understood the difference
between a peaceful home and a home
where abuse dwells. My mother's relief
was palpable. Our next-door neighbor
was an old woman named Dahlie.
Dahlie had Parkinson's. She didn't seem
to have any children or grandchildren. No one
ever came to visit her. Her husband was ex-Air Force
who flew TWA, so he was always gone.
Dahlie was a painter, her walls covered
in pastoral scenes that were exotic to this city kid:
Maud Lewis barns and sheep, windmills,
snowy fields. Her house smelled like coffee
and turpentine. Her easel stood in the corner
of the kitchen, table heaped with tubes of paint,
sketch pads and pencils. For my sixth birthday,
Mom made me a coconut cake decorated with
jellybeans. She had me take a piece to Dahlie.
Dahlie invited me to sit with her while she ate it,
exclaiming over the rainbow colors on white,
pouring me a glass of lemonade. I remember how
the fork trembled in her hand, flakes of coconut
drifting down onto the placemat. She gripped
her brushes in a tight fist. Her paintings shrank
from broad canvases down to postcards. I don't know
if she was ever in a show or if she sold even a single piece.

I used to feel sorry for her, but now I understand
how precious solitude can be for women. That
was the year my mother laughed. For Easter,
she and Dahlie painted eggs together and hid them
in the yard. They shouted *Warmer! Colder!*
as my brother and I searched. Now I understand how,
for the ill, independence matters. You grasp it in your fist
to stop yourself from shaking. You step outside
the world. You invite the exotic into your kitchen.
You eat cake and eggs and summon serenity
with a brushstroke.

Abundance

She's always been a tiny person,
a pixie in childhood,
bright-eyed and bird-boned.
She developed late,
wearing kid's clothes
well into high school.
When she finally needed a bra,
the victory was bittersweet.
Even junior sizes were still
too big, so she had to sew
all her own clothes.

When she became a mother
she found that her breasts
so flowed with milk,
she donated the excess,
proving the adage
about size having nothing
to do with performance,
the breast milk center proceeds
feeding micro preemies
at the NICU.
Her own son was premature,
and she smiles to imagine his
dozens of milk siblings
partaking of her,
understanding only too well
what it's like to be small
and underestimated.

On loving a fat girl

Skinniness is next to godliness,
or so say medieval art of hollow-cheeked
saints and all those runway models
in angel's wings and expensive
lingerie

Earthy is another word for fat,
a back-handed compliment
as all words that try to be fat-positive are

Gluttony a sin
Sensual pleasures a sin
Loving this world a sin

We're supposed to ascend, lighter than air,
to the one beyond
and the robes are not
one-size-fits-all

But what if I want to stay here a while?
What if I want to forego
the land of milk and honey,
preferring instead chocolate and wine?

What if a single God in His single heaven
is not large enough to contain us all?
What if some of us were meant
for pantheons and oh-so forgiving togas?

What if your shame-and-guilt God
has no place in my big fat world?

Fat girl, you
are a magnificent mountain that I want to scale:
the higher the peaks, the lusher the valleys.
You are a sacred grove the gods have smiled on.

There is a body under this robe,
built for more than suffering and motherhood.
There is more than one way to love.
There is more than one way to love the divine.

Snow, Frost, Moon

I get up from the bed
in nothing but my knee socks
and my sex hair, to go stand
at the frosted window pane,
not caring who sees me or if
I catch my death with the sweat
drying to my body. I crack it a bit
and rest my cheek against the ledge,
gulping the icy air, not caring
if anyone knows that we've been
seeking the heat of each other's
cavities, that we've been tied
together in a knot of blankets and
flannel sheets. The nape of my neck
damp, my upper lip glistening
like new snow. Globular December
moon: jizz-white on a black quilt,
celestial money shot pearling
midnight's tits. First, I had to
get warm. Now, I have to
get cold again. How else
will I dive back into bed with you,
how else can I don your skin again?
You could take a handful of snow
and dribble it on my steaming
body, split me open. Season of craving,
that brings to the fore our lust
for salt and fat, for heaviness,

for honey-thick fluids,
for stick-to-your-ribs satisfaction.
I fall back against you and melt
all over the bedding. Outside,
tree branches creak and groan
beneath the weight of their
winter burden, as the mattress
creaks and groans beneath
the weight of us. We must not
waste these long nights.
Silver dawn will find the thrash
of the snow angels we've left behind.

Two Bits

My husband is in the bathroom shaving.
He started wearing a beard at 24,
when he was working in the suit section
of a department store. He found that men
were more comfortable letting him measure
their inseams if he looked less twinkish.
He started balding around the same time. Now,
his hairline is probably somewhere near
the crown of his head. It's hard to say since,
rather than watch the slow retreat of it,
he took to shaving it all off.
Sixteen years later, a ritual has formed:
carefully rolling up the bath mat,
clippers to trim the beard,
electric shaver for his head,
a disposable razor for close work,
Ode to Joy playing on his phone.
Hair that no-color blond that makes it hard
to see the gray coming in, falling in tufts
to the linoleum, hand broom and dustpan
at the ready. He asks me to come
check the back of his head for any
stray patches that he missed. Sometimes,
I take the razor and neaten him up,
kiss the nape of his neck. The mirror
holds us both, neither of us
the high school sweethearts
who first fell in love so we just

have to fall in love again
every day, anew.

After

The bedsheets are pale blue.
In the morning, they are
a disheveled sea,
churned by the tempest
of us.

Light Studies

In art history class, we learned
that Monet would return
to the same spot
over and over again,
working 14 hours a day
no matter the weather,
hoisting his parasol against the wind,
ignoring the icicles whitening his beard,
chasing illumination across wheatfields.
He painted the same pond hundreds of times.
He spent six months in Rouen,
painting nothing but the same cathedral wall,
ten canvases at a time.
A man plagued by radiance,
forever on the edge of conflagration.
In his nightmares,
he is crushed by those pale cathedral stones
and their unattainable hues.
As a teenager living 140 years
after he first picked up a brush,
all I could think was
how dull life must have been in those days,
no television, no radio.
Now, I want nothing more
than a haystack, the waterlilies, sunrises,
an embrace of light;
to be not the capturer,
but the captured,

a stone cracked open,
my light brought forth.

Liminality

First, snow turns to rain. By St. Patrick's Day,
usually, we're in the clear, though I've seen
snow in May. Lent still underway, season of absence,
season of denial, Via Dolorosa yet to be trod.
Now, the tornado siren tests commence.
The ground beneath us warms and softens,
fairy rings of mushrooms appearing in damp yards,
and lichen slicking pedestrian bridges. The invasive
hemlock that looks so harmless at first, so easily
mistaken for ferns along the trails, will spring up
to nine or ten feet before mid-summer, every part of it
toxic; pokeweed garlanded with jewel-bright berries,
also toxic, and dryad's saddle spiraling up tree trunks
where it feasts on the white heart rot. But look,
here is the wild phlox, the wood anemones like stars
at my feet, and the tiny, fragile-stemmed mycena,
a whole galaxy clinging to the root of a decaying tree.
Here is the wild lilac, not yet teeming with bees, its buds
a covenant of petal fragrance to come, that heady mix
of live soil and spring rain that makes it all worth it,
the spear in the side, the rawness and poison. Breathing it in,
it seems impossible to believe the world is anything
but good. Passiontide. Open the windows and air
the place out. Climb the porch railings to hang windchimes.
The ponds awaken, unfurling sheaves of floating duckweed,
frogs singing their aquatic hymns from the creek, the water,
too, crooning over stones. My hands in the soil, my fingers
in the font. I touch them to my forehead, third eye.

Everything open. All the flowering trees, golden forsythia,
cherry, tulip, crabapple, seem to explode all at once,
like fireworks, their petals on sidewalks an after-parade,
a pile of discarded Easter egg shells. The morel hunters
are on the prowl with their sacks, much-needed umami
after forty days of fish and vegetables. The ditches
filled with violets. The irises dramatic with their velvety
dark purples, color of kings and altar cloths and tornadic
skies. Moss flourishes in the cracks of limestone bluffs.
Everywhere, tombs opening. Everywhere, eggs and seeds
cracking open. Hemisphere tilting sunward. On our knees,
in the garden, pouring from a bottle of Easter water.
The tornado sirens sound and, unafraid, we go
take shelter in the earth.

Solace

My favorite apartment was
by Cathedral Square,
the church founded in 1835,
a log cabin overlooking the river.
Its first parishioners would have been
farmers and traders,
maybe a fur trapper or two,
though they don't strike me
as the praying type.

Now, its golden steeple
presides over a bustling downtown.
How I loved awakening to its great bells,
lauds and vespers underscored by light;
the tower that's burnished at sunset
glints at dawn. I used to think
that I was not worthy
to receive such solace,
that beginnings and endings do not
have to be so dreadful.

Innocence

We used to play
in the alleys and vacant lots,
robins, titmice and mourning doves
dotting the power lines.
The feral cats we always
tried to capture and tame,
wanting something
to call our own.
Bare feet in the uncut grass,
splashing in the kiddie pool.
Water cold from the hose,
backyard baptisms,
imagining our souls
as pure as the green world
fluttering and scurrying
around us.

Publication Notes

These poems have appeared or are forthcoming in: *Lucifer's Retreat, The Rye Whiskey Review, Life and Legends, Fleas on the Dog, Curating Home, Madness Muse Press, Levitate Magazine, BigCityLit, Setu Magazine, Arkana, New Feathers, Sledgehammer Literary Journal* (UK), *PØST* (Canada), *Ordinary Madness, The Black Shamrock Magazine, Unlikely Stories - Mark V, The Dope Fiend Daily, Pocket Lint, Stone Poetry Quarterly, Stanzaic Stylings, Gone but Not Forgotten* Anthology, *From the Ashes, Wraparound South, Anvil Tongue Press, Artifact Nouveau, Libretto Magazine* (Nigeria), *Plainsongs, The Racket, Heroin Love Songs, Written Tales Magazine, The Argyle,* and *Bards of a Feather* Anthology (India).

"A Seat at the Table" was nominated for a Best of the Net. "Confection" was nominated for a Pushcart Prize.

Lauren Scharhag (she/her) is a queer, disabled author of Latine descent, and a senior editor at *Gleam*. To date, her work includes poetry, horror, science-fiction, fantasy, children's books, and literary fiction. She hopes to add to the list. She is extensively published in literary venues around the world. Recent honors include: 2023 Rhysling Award Finalist, 2022 SFFP Speculative Poetry Contest (Honorable Mention), 2021 Stephen A. DiBiase Poetry Contest (Finalist), and the 2019 Seamus Burns Creative Writing Prize (Winner). Her work has also received multiple Best of the Net, Pushcart Prize, and Rhysling Award nominations. Her latest poetry collection, *Moonlight and Monsters*, is now available from Gnashing Teeth Publishing. A short story collection, *Screaming Intensifies*, is forthcoming from Whiskey City Press. She lives in Kansas City, MO.

https://linktr.ee/laurenscharhag

MORE ROADSIDE PRESS TITLES:

By Plane, Train or Coincidence
Michele McDannold

Prying
Jack Micheline, Charles Bukowski and Catfish McDaris

Wolf Whistles Behind the Dumpster
Dan Provost

Busking Blues: Recollections of a Chicago Street Musician and Squatter
Westley Heine

Unknowable Things
Kerry Trautman

How to Play House
Heather Dorn

Kiss the Heathens
Ryan Quinn Flanagan

St. James Infirmary
Steven Meloan

Street Corner Spirits
Westley Heine

A Room Above a Convenience Store
William Taylor Jr.

Resurrection Song
George Wallace

Nothing and Too Much to Talk About
Nancy Patrice Davenport

Bar Guide for the Seriously Deranged
Alan Catlin

MORE ROADSIDE PRESS TITLES:

Born on Good Friday
Nathan Graziano

Under Normal Conditions
Karl Koweski

The Dead and the Desperate
Dan Denton

Clown Gravy
Misti Rainwater-Lites

Walking Away
Michael D. Grover

All in a Pretty Little Row
Dan Provost

These Are the People in Your Neighbourhood
Jordan Trethewey

They Said I Wasn't College Material
Scot Young

Radio Water
Francine Witte

And Blackberries Grew Wild
Susan Mickelberry

Licorice Heart
Miles Budimir

Disposable Darlings
Todd Cirillo

Full Moon Midnight
Belinda Subraman

MORE ROADSIDE PRESS TITLES:

Innocent Postcards
John Pietaro

Cistern Latitudes
James Duncan

Another Saturday Night in Jukebox Hell
Alan Catlin

Abandoned By All Things
Karl Koweski